*Our thanks are due to Steven Arthur
for his expert advice.*

ISBN 1 85103 117 0

First published 1990 by Editions Gallimard
First published 1991 in Great Britain by Moonlight Publishing Ltd,
36 Stratford Road, London W8
© 1990 Editions Gallimard
English text © 1991 Moonlight Publishing Ltd

Printed in Italy by Editoriale Libraria

MODERN AIRCRAFT

| DISCOVERERS |

Written and illustrated by
James Prunier

Translated by Margaret Malpas

MOONLIGHT PUBLISHING

Contents

- 8 **Modern airliners**
  The rivalry between
  Boeing and Douglas
- 10 **A range of airliners**
  From 1964 onward
- 12 **The Airbus**
  A European aircraft
- 14 **Building an airliner**
  The magic of flight
- 16 **Airline insignia**
- 18 **Airports and
  air-traffic control**
  Take-off and landing
- 20 **Learning to fly**
  Aircraft and helicopters
- 22 **Business and pleasure**
  Civil aviation
- 24 **Rescue missions**
  Water-bombers
  and air-ambulances
- 26 **Gliding**
  Flying without an engine
- 28 **Parachuting and free-falling**
- 30 **Balloons**
  Around the world in 80 days . . .
- 32 **Airshows**
  Performance-flying
- 34 **Learner pilots**
  A rigorous discipline
- 36 **Air forces and insignia**
- 38 **The jet age**
  Modern developments
- 40 **Bombers**
  The nuclear threat
- 42 **Helicopters in combat**
  Algeria, Vietnam,
  Afghanistan
- 44 **Transport aircraft**
- 46 **Aircraft-carriers**
- 48 **Modern war-planes**
- 50 **Spy planes**
- 52 **Crazy planes**
  Vertical take-off
- 54 **In-flight refuelling**
- 56 **Through the sound
  to the heat barrier**
  Chuck Yeager
- 58 **Supersonic airliners**
  Concorde and the
  Tupolev Tu-144
- 60 **Dreaming of space**
  Truth or fiction
- 62 **In orbit**
  Rockets and satellites
- 64 **Apollo 11**
  Mission to the moon
- 66 **Men on the moon**
  Armstrong and Aldrin
- 68 **Space-shuttles**
  A ferry service to
  the stars
- 70 **The space-travellers**
- 72 **An A to Z of aircraft facts**
- 76 **About the author**

Modern airliners

By the 1960s the two American rivals, Boeing and Douglas, controlled the world's airliner production. Both companies developed a range of passenger aircraft which they sold to airlines around the globe, transforming the industry.

Boeing and Douglas produced mainly long-haul craft which left room for other aircraft companies, especially European companies, to continue to develop short and medium-haul planes. But it was the contribution of Boeing and Douglas, and their long-haul craft, which caused the drop in ticket prices and made air travel accessible to everyone.

Douglas DC-10

The Boeing 247 first produced in 1933 was followed by the 707, 727, 737 and the famous 747.

Airliners are classified as long-haul, medium-haul or short-haul, according to the distance they can travel without refuelling. This distance varies from under 2,000 km, for the Hawker Siddeley Trident, to over 10,000 km for a Boeing 747.

A range of airliners

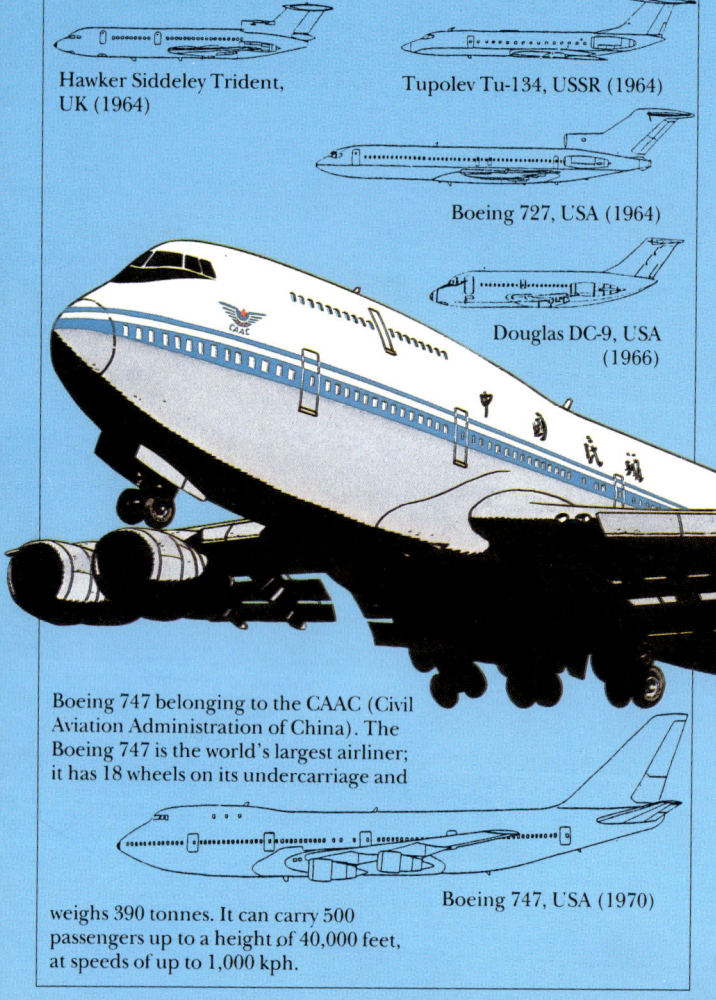

Hawker Siddeley Trident, UK (1964)

Tupolev Tu-134, USSR (1964)

Boeing 727, USA (1964)

Douglas DC-9, USA (1966)

Boeing 747 belonging to the CAAC (Civil Aviation Administration of China). The Boeing 747 is the world's largest airliner; it has 18 wheels on its undercarriage and weighs 390 tonnes. It can carry 500 passengers up to a height of 40,000 feet, at speeds of up to 1,000 kph.

Boeing 747, USA (1970)

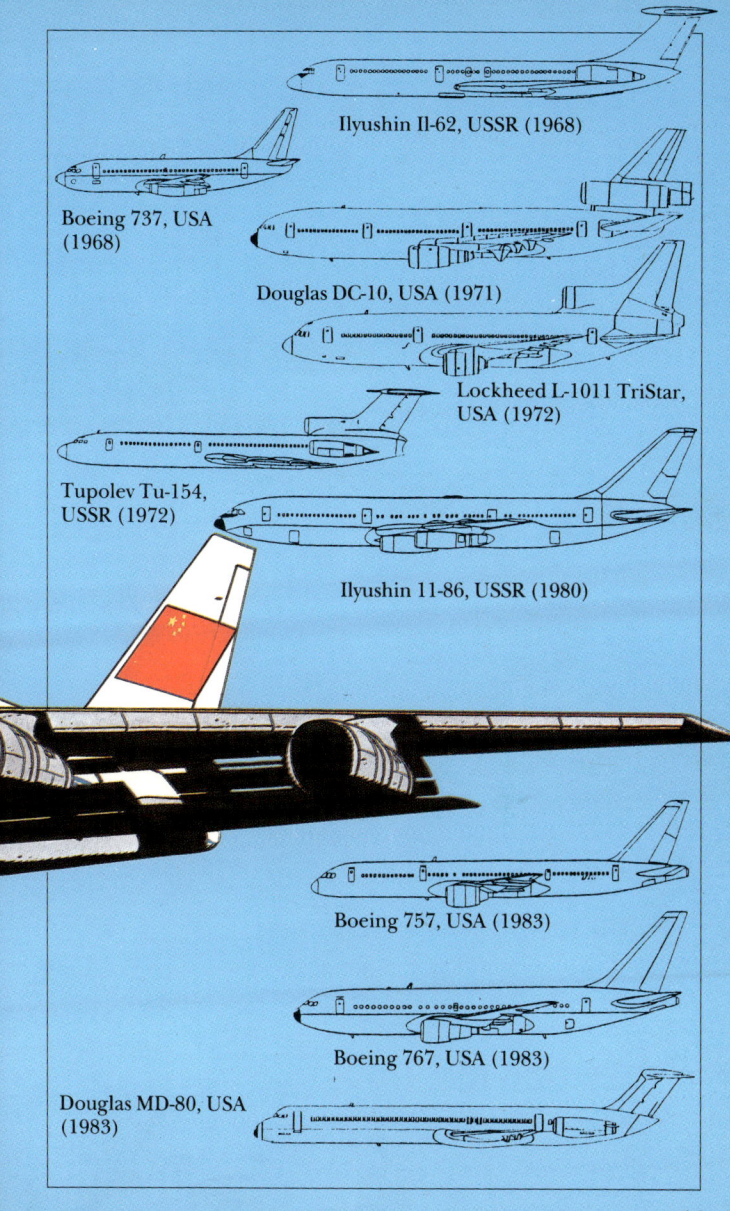

The Airbus

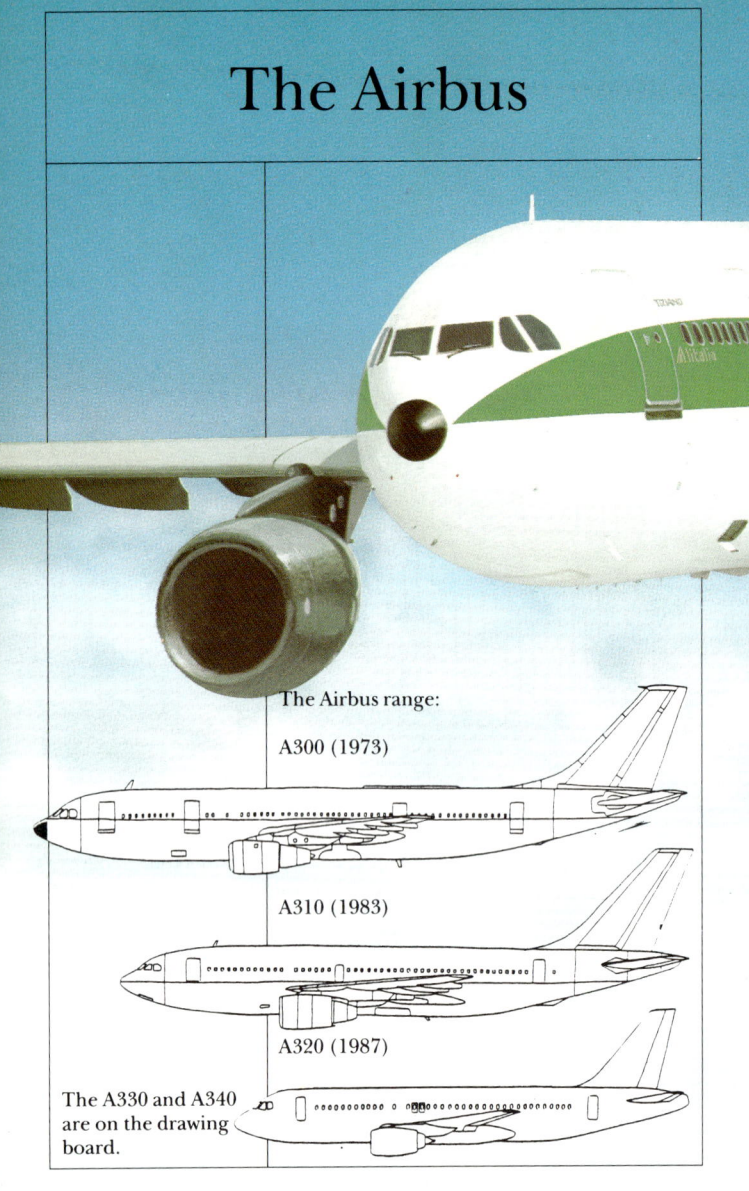

The Airbus range:

A300 (1973)

A310 (1983)

A320 (1987)

The A330 and A340 are on the drawing board.

Airbus A330

Since 1983, traditional twin-engined jets designed for economy, such as the Boeing 757 and 767, the Douglas MD-80 and the Airbus, have used the most up-to-date technology.

The Airbus, the joint project of a group of European countries, is now posing a serious threat to the American airliners.

Different countries provide the various sections of the A320.

- France
- West Germany
- Spain
- Britain
- Belgium
- USA

Building an airliner

Airliners are not all the same. The jet engines can be put in different places, and the tailplane can be mounted in various positions.

The wing of an Airbus is tested for signs of stress.

In a small back room, designers and engineers plan a new aircraft; but years pass before it can be put into service. First, models have to be tested in a wind-tunnel, to see how they behave

Structure of a wing

The picture shows how an aircraft's wing appears when landing. The leading and trailing-edge flaps extend to help produce more lift at high speed.
1. Air-flow
2. Leading-edge flaps
3. Outer aileron
4. Inner aileron
5. Trailing-edge flap
6. Air-brake
7. Fuel-tank

14

in flight. Then a series of full-size prototypes are built, and put through all sorts of tests designed to show up any weaknesses. Once all the faults have been ironed out, the aircraft can enter service.

Some aircraft designs are very flexible. The Boeing 747 can be built as a passenger plane, a cargo plane, or a mixture of the two, like the one shown here.

The magic of flight
As an aircraft flies along air moves past its wings. The shape of the wings forces air to flow over them more quickly then below them. This creates an area of higher pressure below the wings which causes lift (1).

The more curved the wings are, the faster the air is forced to flow over them. The difference in air-pressure is increased and this in turn creates more lift.

The narrow wings of the airliners are designed to be efficient at high cruising speeds. At lower speeds, on take-off and landing; lift is increased by using flaps made of movable parts, which make the surface area of the wing larger and more curved.

When the aircraft is ready to land, the air-brakes are also used.

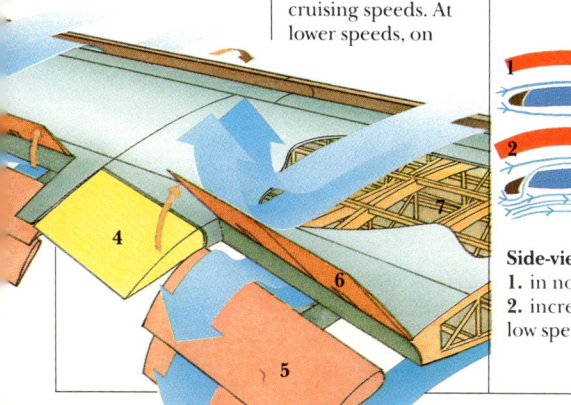

Side-view of a wing:
1. in normal flight
2. increasing lift for low speeds

Airline insignia

Air Jamaica
Aeromexico
Alaska Airlines
Egyptair
Air India

In the late 1920s, the directors of some airlines decided to paint distinctive signs on their passenger cabins, so that the aircraft could easily be identified with the airlines and could serve as advertisements for them.

Soon everyone else followed suit, and all fuselages carried the company's name and sign.

Aero Peru
Aerolineas Argentinas
Air New-Zealand
PIA (Pakistan)
Surinam Airways
Air Gabon

Rival companies also tried to outdo each other in the elegance of their internal decor, the comfort of their aircraft, the quality of their service and the smartness of the crew's uniforms. Some airlines now ask top designers to plan their planes' colour-schemes and design the uniforms.

In 1973, the American company Braniff commissioned Alexander Calder, an artist famous for designing mobiles, to decorate the fuselage of one of its DC-8s.

Airports and air-traffic control

Roissy-Charles-de-Gaulle, 27 km from Paris. The central building links seven terminals, each of which can take four jumbo-jets at a time. Telescopic gangways enable passengers to walk from the terminals right into the aircraft.

Landing

Still travelling at about 300 kph, the aircraft approaches the runway at an angle of 3°.
1. At a height of 70 ft, the pilot throttles back to reduce speed and pulls up the nose of the aircraft.
2. The main wheels of the undercarriage touch down first, at 230 kph.
3. Then the nose-wheel touches down. The aircraft is now travelling on the ground, and the pilot applies reverse thrust from the engines to act as a brake.

When jet-powered airliners came into general use, bigger airports were needed to handle the ever-increasing traffic.

Air-traffic control
At busy airports, the aircraft wait for permission to land.

The Instrument Landing System (ILS) helps them approach the airport. Radio beams guide the pilots down towards their allotted runway.

Recently a new system has been developed. The Microwave Landing System (MLS) can guide numerous aircraft from different directions into the airport at the same time. This naturally allows the airport to handle a much greater volume of traffic. However, at present this system is not in widespread use.

A Boeing 727 on its final approach

An air-traffic controller's job is to keep aircraft at a safe distance from one another, all the time that they are in the air, and to guide them to their destinations.

Controllers are technicians. They use radar screens to monitor aircraft, and they are in permanent radio contact with the pilot and his crew.

Take-off

1. The aircraft is stationary until all final checks have been made. The brakes are released when the staff in the control-tower give the order. The pilot applies full power, and the aircraft gathers speed.
2. At 300 kph the aircraft's nose lifts from the ground.
3. The aircraft rises into the air at the correct climb angle.

Learning to fly

Forces at work
1. Lift
2. Weight
3. Thrust
4. Drag

Whether you are flying a huge airliner or a small plane, the principles of flight are exactly the same. The three movements are pitching, rolling and yawing. A pilot has to learn to co-ordinate these movements smoothly and accurately to make the aircraft turn, or move up or down. At the same time, he must keep an eye on all the dials on the instrument panel.

Artificial horizon
An instrument on the panel shows the exact angle of the aircraft (the fixed white shape) in relation to the ground.
The artificial horizon on the screen moves so that it is always parallel with the ground.

Controlling flight
Pitching is controlled by the elevator (**1**), which is attached to the joystick; rolling by the ailerons (**2**), also attached to the joystick; and yawing by the rudder (**3**), operated by the rudder-bar. The engine is controlled by the throttle, which works like the accelerator in a car.

lift

rotation

Pitch of the rotor: this can be changed (pink arrows) to make the helicopter fly forwards, backwards or sideways. It is controlled by the red cyclic stick.

Pitch of each rotor-blade: changing this (blue arrows) alters the amount of air being disturbed, and so increases or reduces lift, making the helicopter rise or fall. The blue collective-pitch lever controls this.

Helicopters also have three main controls, which regulate the pitch of the whole rotor, the pitch of each blade of the rotor, and yawing.

Yawing: the couple effect (**1**) set up by the main rotor (**2**) would make the helicopter spin helplessly in the air were it not for the small tail-rotor (**3**). The green rudder-pedal alters the angle of the tail-rotor, which changes the horizontal direction of flight.

21

Business and pleasure

As well as the airlines and the armed forces, all sorts of organizations and individuals fly aircraft, both for pleasure and for business. In remote areas, aircraft are used to carry goods and take people to hospital. Farmers use small craft to spray crops.

Private flying became popular in the 1930s with the arrival of the De Havilland Moth, and the first flying clubs were founded. Private pilots usually fly small planes with one or two engines. The earliest models had a wooden or metal framework covered in cloth, but modern aircraft are made of light alloys or of fibreglass.

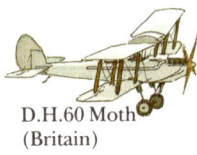

D.H.60 Moth (Britain)

Cessna 150 (USA)

Piper Cherokee (USA)

Beechcraft A-60 Duke (USA)

The Dassault Falcon 900, which can carry 19 passengers at 930 kph, and fly 7,400 km without refuelling (France)

Business aircraft nowadays are usually jet-propelled, so that they can travel faster and further.

In the developed world, light aircraft are now part of everyday life. There are airfields all around where it is often possible to learn how to fly. You can even buy a kit and build an aeroplane yourself.

Crop-spraying aircraft are very useful for anyone trying to farm a large area.

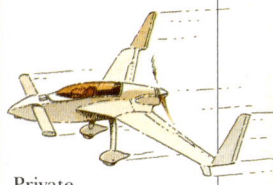

Private aeroplane

The executive jet is just another office for its owner.

Helicopters are also commonly used for all sorts of non-military purposes. They are extremely useful because they are able to land almost anywhere: on an oil-rig at sea, for instance, or even on the flat roof of an office-block in the middle of a city, where a plane couldn't land.

Half hang-glider, half aircraft, the micro-light is a sort of flying motorbike. It is really only a pleasure craft but in 1986 the French pilot Patrice Franceschi flew a micro-light round the world, and in 1987 Nicolas Hulot and Hubert de Chevigny flew one over the North Pole.

Rescue missions

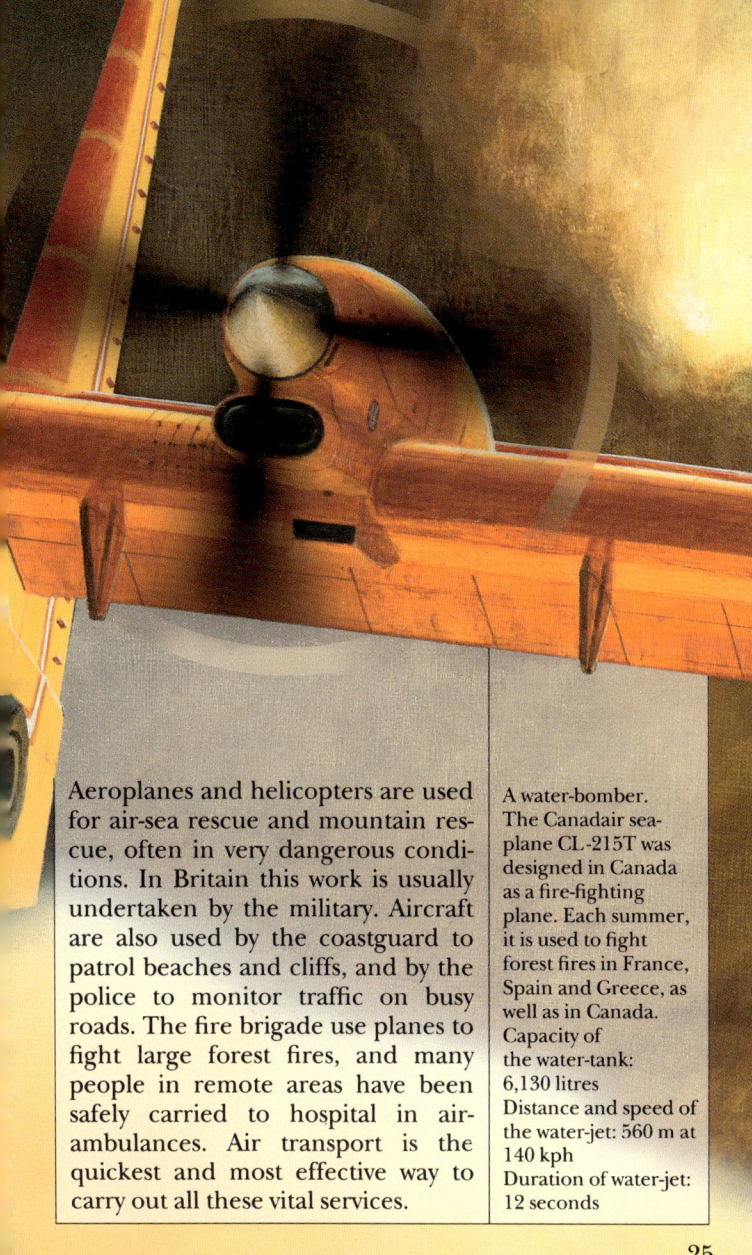

Aeroplanes and helicopters are used for air-sea rescue and mountain rescue, often in very dangerous conditions. In Britain this work is usually undertaken by the military. Aircraft are also used by the coastguard to patrol beaches and cliffs, and by the police to monitor traffic on busy roads. The fire brigade use planes to fight large forest fires, and many people in remote areas have been safely carried to hospital in air-ambulances. Air transport is the quickest and most effective way to carry out all these vital services.

A water-bomber. The Canadair seaplane CL-215T was designed in Canada as a fire-fighting plane. Each summer, it is used to fight forest fires in France, Spain and Greece, as well as in Canada.
Capacity of the water-tank: 6,130 litres
Distance and speed of the water-jet: 560 m at 140 kph
Duration of water-jet: 12 seconds

Gliding

Slope soaring makes use of the regular, rising air-currents which are usually found above mountain slopes.

Thermal soaring makes use of the currents of hot air rising above surfaces which have been heated by the sun (roofs in a town, for instance). A really skilled pilot can also use the pockets of warm air under cumulus clouds to soar to a considerable height.

Gliders

In 1864 the French pilot Louis Mouillard (1834–97) flew a glider he had designed himself. After watching vultures soaring over the desert in Egypt and Algeria he became convinced that the best way to fly was with wings like sails which simply used the forces present in the atmosphere. He invented the technique of banking, which was later used by the Wrights.

In 1921 the German pilot Leusch found out how to use warm air-currents, called thermals, to rise in the air.

Louis Mouillard in his 'sailing monoplane' No.4 (1895)

Today, the altitude record for a glider stands at 43,700 feet (Bickle, USA, 25 February 1961). The distance record is 1,460 km (Grosse, Germany, 25 April 1972).

Hang-gliders

These were a development from the original gliders. Their modern triangular shape was conceived by the American designer Francis Rogallo.

To steer the machine, the pilot shifts the weight of his body by moving the triangular metal framework which supports him.

A hang-glider pilot lies flat, with the lower half of his body in a sort of bag. The smooth shape reduces drag.

Modern gliders are made of fibreglass. They are very light and streamlined, with the largest possible wing surface.

Glider taking off, towed by an aeroplane

Climbing

Free flight

Parachuting and free-falling

A parachute consists of a canopy, made of strong light-weight material, and a number of suspension-lines, the ropes joining the canopy to the parachutist's harness. Steering-lines direct the parachute and compensate for the effects of the wind.

There are two different systems for opening a parachute. It can be opened automatically by a cable fixed to the aircraft, or the parachutist can pull the ripcord when he has reached a suitable height.

The way the parachutist lands on the ground depends on the speed at which he is travelling, the strength and direction of the wind, and the angle at which he approaches the landing-place. He may be able to land on his feet, or he may have to roll over on the ground. In a parachuting competition, the aim is to land as near as possible to the centre of a target.

Paragliding

The paraglider looks like a parachute, but is based on the principle of the hang-glider. The 'sail' is made of tubes which fill with air, so that the pilot can take off from the top of a slope and glide downwards. This sport is usually practised in the mountains.

Free-falling is controlled by the position of the body; at 180 kph, even the smallest movement of a hand can alter the direction in which you fall. In competitions, free-fall parachutists have to adopt various positions for which they win points. The free-fall parachutist's most important piece of equipment is his altimeter, which warns him as he approaches 60 m. At that height he must pull the cord to open his parachute. The world free-fall record of 76,000 feet was set by the Russian Andreev in 1962.

The women's record of 46,000 feet was set by another Russian, Fomitcheva.

Balloons

The best time for ballooning is in the early morning or the evening, when the air is cooler and the winds are light. The cloth canopy attached to the wicker basket, or gondola, slowly unfolds as cold air is pumped into it. When it is time to start, the burner above the gondola is turned on to heat the air inside the canopy. The burner is fuelled by liquid propane, and on a pleasure flight there is usually enough fuel to last for about two hours.

The balloon rises because it is filled with hot air but $1m^3$ of hot air only lifts about 300 g, and the balloon has to be huge to raise even the weight of the gondola. The air inside must be about 70° Celsius hotter than the surrounding air to lift the balloon from the ground. If the temperature is 20° Celsius, the air in the canopy has to be kept at 90° Celsius. At the top of the canopy is a valve, controlled from the gondola, through which hot air can escape. By regulating the amount of air in the canopy, the balloonist controls the speed at which the balloon rises or falls. The same valve is used to deflate the canopy after landing. All balloonists today carry radios, to contact the vehicle which will retrieve them when the balloon has landed.

Ballooning rallies and competitions are held regularly. The most famous takes place every October in Albuquerque, New Mexico.

Airshows

Aerobatic manoeuvres

horizontal roll

looping the loop

loop and roll

turn and roll

stall turn

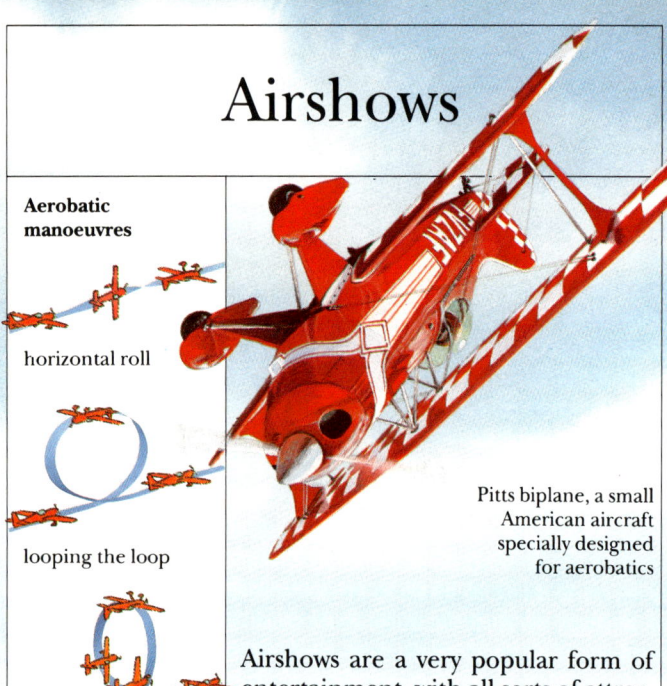

Pitts biplane, a small American aircraft specially designed for aerobatics

Airshows are a very popular form of entertainment, with all sorts of attractions for aircraft enthusiasts: demonstrations of new civil and military planes, mock battles, aerobatics and formation flying. On the ground, visitors can see everything from vintage aircraft to the latest technology.

Aircraft designed to perform aerobatics have extra strong frames, to enable them to withstand the huge forces which occur during some of the manoeuvres. Their powerful engines have special fuel and oil systems which allow the planes to fly upside down.

The pilots have harnesses to keep them safely in their seats, and often wear parachutes too.

The pilots combine the basic loops, rolls and spins in an infinite number of ways, performing extraordinary aerial ballets. The most fantastic manoeuvre, the Lomcevak, involves a series of stunts and ends with the aeroplane tumbling end over end through the sky.

The French display team

National display teams are made up of pilots trained to carry out all kinds of feats. These pilots subject themselves to immense centrifugal forces and grave danger, for the thrill of performing their stunts at high speeds in powerful aircraft.

Aerobatics at La Ferté-Alais, at the 1988 airshow

The British team, the Red Arrows, flying in formation

The American air force team, the Thunderbirds, fly F16 Fighting Falcons

A spectacular stunt by the Italian team, the Frecce Tricolori

Learner pilots

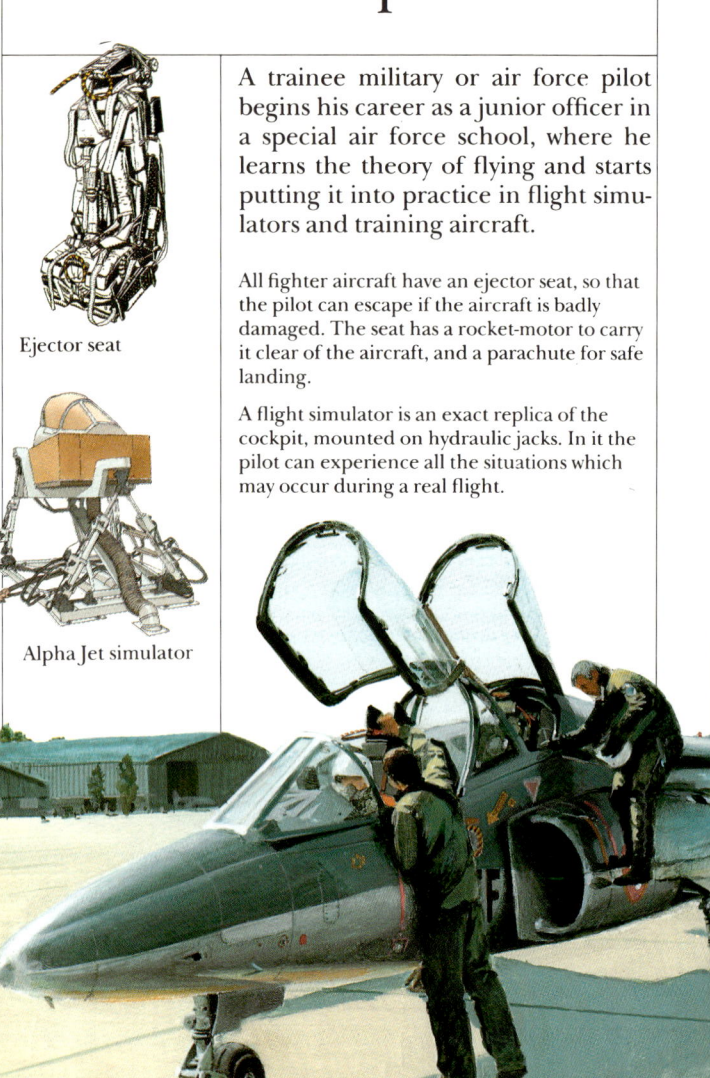

Ejector seat

Alpha Jet simulator

A trainee military or air force pilot begins his career as a junior officer in a special air force school, where he learns the theory of flying and starts putting it into practice in flight simulators and training aircraft.

All fighter aircraft have an ejector seat, so that the pilot can escape if the aircraft is badly damaged. The seat has a rocket-motor to carry it clear of the aircraft, and a parachute for safe landing.

A flight simulator is an exact replica of the cockpit, mounted on hydraulic jacks. In it the pilot can experience all the situations which may occur during a real flight.

Before a training flight, the pilot has a briefing session. He listens to the weather forecast, studies the flight charts and ground maps and makes certain he knows which air-space is available for military use, so that he does not stray into air-corridors reserved for airlines. After the flight there is a de-briefing session, in which the pilot analyses his flight and discusses ways of improving his performance.

When a student has completed his training, he is posted to an air force unit as a fully-fledged pilot.

Alpha Jets flying in formation.
The Alpha Jet is made jointly by Dassault-Breguet (France) and Dornier (Germany).

Student pilot dressed for flying at high altitudes. He wears an anti-G flying-suit, and carries an oxygen mask. In his pockets are maps and charts.

Alpha Jet training aircraft. The student sits at the front; his instructor sits behind, where he can operate the dual controls.

Air forces and insignia

Air forces are stationed at operational bases. In addition countries with nuclear weapons have special bases for tactical and strategic forces.

The role of the air force in wartime is well-known, but they also do important peace-time work. They patrol the skies above their own countries, and above the lands of their allies, ready to intercept any enemy planes which intrude into the airspace. The air forces also ensure that vital air-corridors are kept open, so that food and other supplies can be brought in during an emergency.

Various types of specialized aircraft have to be kept ready for different purposes: to intercept possible intruders, and for rescue missions, surveillance, reconnaissance, and even spying.

Sheep sometimes graze peacefully on the vast areas of grassland on air force bases.

Large flocks of birds on an airfield can easily cause accidents, so falcons and hawks are used to chase away other birds.

Guard-dogs are used for airfield security.

The jet age

Production of military aircraft did not stop at the end of the Second World War. It remains a massive industry.

The major powers export their military technology, so that even small localized conflicts may involve the firepower of MiGs, Sabres, Mirages or Phantoms.

The sophisticated weaponry and specialized equipment of modern

The Mikoyan-Gurevich MiG-15 (1948), a high-altitude fighter, is the best known of the early Russian jets.

English Electric Lightning (1959) This British fighter with its swept-back wings has two jets, one above the other, though it needs only one for cruising.

fighters are constantly refined and improved. They include radar systems which locate an enemy's exact position, and heat-seeking missiles

Lockheed F-104 Starfighter (1958) This American fighter, with its short wings and narrow body, looks rather like a rocket. Altitude record 98,000 feet.

which home in on the hot engine of an enemy plane. The most powerful modern fighters can reach speeds of over 2,000 kph, and altitudes of 60,000 feet.

Dassault Mirage IIIE (1964) French delta-wing fighter.

Saab AJ 37 Viggen Thunderbolt (1976) Swedish delta-wing fighter. To increase efficiency, the elevators are situated at the front, and the tail is high.

Bombers

Oceans are no longer an obstacle for the big bombers. Modern planes can travel vast distances without refuelling (12,500 km for a Russian Tupolev Tu-142) and can be used in

Convair B-36
(USA, 1948)

action far away from their home base.

The first aircraft to fly non-stop right round the world was the Boeing B-50 turbo-prop bomber *Lucky Lady II*. The flight lasted from

Boeing B-52
Stratofortress
(USA, 1955)

29 February to 2 March 1949. Refuelling took place in the air by attaching a pipe from a tanker to the bomber's fuel-tanks.

Jet bombers were the next stage:

Tupolev Tu-95,
known to NATO as
Bear-D
(USSR, 1956)

on 26 August 1952 an English Electric Canberra was the first to fly both ways across the Atlantic in a single day.

A bomber armed for a mission can trans-

port an enormous load. A Boeing B-52 can carry 31,750 kg of bombs; a Rockwell B-1B can carry 24 short-range nuclear missiles.

Nuclear weapons aboard strategic bombers

Avro Vulcan
(Britain, 1957)

are carried either in the fuselage or under the wings. The weapons are often cruise missiles, which are programmed to fall on a specific target, reducing the risk of human error.

Dassault Mirage IV
(France, 1964)

Inter-continental nuclear missiles may also be ground-based or carried in submarines. Nuclear weapons are said to be a deterrent to war, because no one dares risk a nuclear

Tupolev Tu-26
Backfire
(USSR, 1969)

attack. But possessing nuclear power has become a sign of a nation's strength, and there are now enough nuclear missiles and bombs to destroy our planet many times over.

Rockwell
International B-1B
(USA, 1984)

Helicopters in combat

Vertol-Piasecki H-21 Banana

Sikorsky H-34

Helicopters have played an important part in combat since the Second World War. Their manoeuvrability and vertical take-off and landing make them useful as back-up for the men on the frontline. They can be used to land troops quickly where they are needed, and to bring rapid medical aid to the wounded. When the French were involved in the conflict in **Algeria** (1954–62) helicopters proved very effective. They were used to drop supplies, to ferry out the wounded, to transport troops into and out of the battle-zone, and to tackle the problem of guerrilla warfare.

*The airplane won't amount to a damn
until they get a machine
that will act like a humming-bird –
go straight up, go forward,
come straight down and alight . . .*
Thomas Edison

Boeing Vertol CH-47 Chinook

Bell HU-1 Iroquois Huey

During the war in **Vietnam** (1965–75) the Americans set up special airborne units to attack guerrillas in the jungle. Fast, manoeuvrable helicopter gunships were ideally suited to these missions, and reached areas that would otherwise have been quite inaccessible.

During the **Afghanistan** war (1979-89) the Russians used their armed assault and gunship helicopter, the MIL-Mi-24 (NATO code-name Hind).

Transport aircraft

Antonov AN-225 Mriya (USSR)
Designed in 1985. Load: 250 tonnes.

The Lockheed C-5A Galaxy and C-130 Hercules were amongst the transporters used by the Allies during the Gulf War (1991). Some of the C-130s were also adapted for low level flying under combat conditions.

Lockheed C-5A Galaxy (USA)
Built in 1963. Load: 120 tonnes.

Short Belfast (Britain) Built in 1964.
Load: 36 tonnes.

Lockheed C-130 Hercules (USA)
Built in 1962. Load: 200 tonnes.

Nord Aviation/Hamburger und Weser
Transall C-160 (France/Germany)
Built in 1963. Load: 15 tonnes.

Boeing 747 (USA)

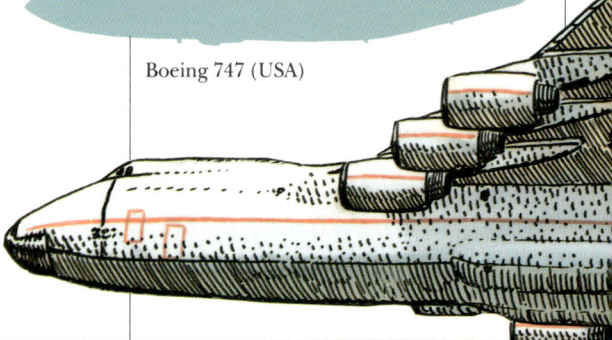

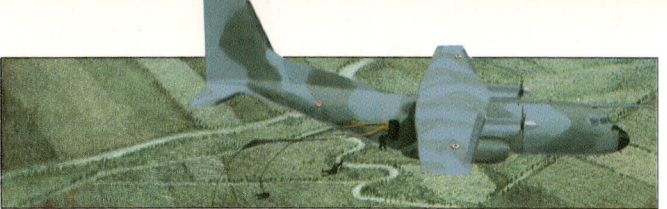

A modern army has to be able to transport large numbers of troops and vast quantities of equipment anywhere in the world. Diplomatic operations require the capability of moving officials and supplies rapidly and at short notice.

Today all major powers have transport fleets which range from luxurious high speed jets to enormous personnel and cargo carriers, with huge holds, specially designed to meet the demands of military administrators. The three basic types of military transport aeroplanes are the short-haul aircraft used over short distances, medium-range tactical aircraft and long-range strategic aircraft.

Parachute drop by a Transall C160, which can cruise at 500 kph with its full load of 15 tonnes.

The huge nose of the Galaxy is raised to swallow up the cargo.

An-225 Mriya
Wingspan: 88.4 m
Length: 84 m
Height: 18.1 m
Maximum gross weight: 600 tonnes
Load: 250 tonnes
Maximum cruising speed: 950 kph
Range with 200 tonnes load: 4,500 km

Aircraft-carriers

1. Directing take-off
2. Directing landing
3. The fireman stands by in case there is an emergency.

A crew-member with a set of signal lights guides the pilot down.

The aeroplanes transported on Second World War aircraft-carriers all had conventional propeller engines. The first jet aeroplane to land on an aircraft-carrier was the Ryan FR-1 Fireball turbo-prop, which Lieutenant Jack C. West landed on the deck of the American vessel *Wake Island* on 6 November 1945.

Since then, aircraft-carriers have become more sophisticated. They have angled flight decks, steam-driven catapults to help jets take off, and a mirror to help with landing. They can also carry missile-intercepting planes used to protect submarines.

An aircraft-carrier is just like a floating town, with a hospital, its own local television station, and various churches. A big aircraft-carrier may have as many as 4,600 men in its crew, each with his own special work to do.

The short runways on aircraft-carriers make landing and take-off particularly difficult. The plane takes off under its own power, although a raised ramp at the end of the runway is sometimes used to increase lift. After the flight the pilot has to land at 250 kph on a short runway which rises and falls with the movement of the waves. He also has to hook his aircraft on to one of the wires stretched across the deck, to prevent the plane from speeding off the end of the runway into the sea.

To land successfully, the pilot must get everything right: the speed, the angle of descent, and the angle at which the plane hits the deck.

Planes are launched from various positions (the red arrows in the picture) and land on the angled deck (the yellow arrow).

American Grumman F-14 Tomcat fighter

The French Dassault-Breguet Rafale has its elevators in front of the wings to make it more manoeuvrable.

Nowadays the battle for air superiority is fought out by the new generation of fighter planes, made of special alloys and equipped with sophisticated electronic equipment to control an array of offensive and defensive weapons. Though they fly only a little faster than the fighters of the previous generation, they are much more efficient.

The first air-battles were restricted by the planes' limited manoeuvrability. Today, aircraft can achieve acceleration up to 9G, and equally rapid deceleration. Pilots must try to anticipate the enemy's tactics, because the battle only lasts a few moments.

Russian Mikoyan-Gurevich MiG-29 fighter

Swing-wings
Some fighters have movable wings which alter the plane's shape to increase its speed. At low speeds the wings are spread wide to give lift; at high speeds they are folded in to reduce drag.

European Panavia Tornado fighter, with movable swing-wings.

The American General Dynamics F-16 Fighting Falcon fighter gives the pilot unobstructed vision all the way round.

Modern war-planes

Spy-planes

American Lockheed SR-71 Blackbird (1966) The Blackbird is the best of the specialized strategic reconnaissance aircraft. As it flies along at 76,000 feet, at a speed of Mach 3, its probes can survey an area of 135,000 km² every hour. It refuels in the air, outside the surveillance zone.

The U-2 affair
On 1 May 1960, during the Cold War, an American pilot called Gary Powers was on a routine flight over the USSR, in his Lockheed U-2, when a ground-to-air missile struck his aircraft. Powers baled out but was taken prisoner when he landed. He was released in 1962, the year another U-2 was shot down by the Cubans.
Today, U-2s are used by American geographers and geologists to study their own country.

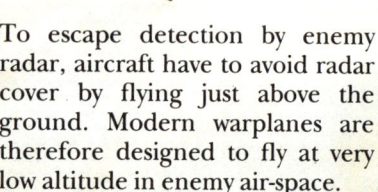

To escape detection by enemy radar, aircraft have to avoid radar cover by flying just above the ground. Modern warplanes are therefore designed to fly at very low altitude in enemy air-space.

A strategic reconnaissance aircraft flies very high and very fast, to

avoid being intercepted. Reconnaissance is also carried out by spy satellites sent up into space.

Cruise missiles can be fired from planes operating well outside the enemy airspace. The missiles, which can be equipped with nuclear warheads, fly low to avoid radar detection, following the contours of the ground until they reach their target.

'Stealth' fighters and bombers avoid detection in an entirely new way. Their design and construction make them completely invisible on a radar screen.

Lockheed F-117 fighter, operational in 1989

Northrop B-2 strategic bomber, which first flew in July 1989.

These are both American Stealth aircraft. The F-117 was used most recently in the Gulf war (1991).

Crazy planes

Flying wings
One of the few successful flying-wing designs was built by the American company Northrop.

Northrop YB-49 'flying wing' with eight jets

Their MX-324, propelled by a rocket-engine, flew in 1944. Next came the propeller-driven wing XB-35 (1946), followed by the jet-propelled YV-49. The US Army ordered 35 of these machines to use as bombers and for remote reconnaissance, but then the order was withdrawn and the makers were ordered to destroy the prototype. They were very reluctant to do this because they believed, both then and later, that the plane could have revolutionized the design of transport aircraft.

Vertical take-off and landing
Designers wanted to create an aircraft which combined the vertical take-off properties of a helicopter with the speed and efficiency of a fixed-wing aeroplane.

1. American Convair XFY-1 Pogo (1954) This was the first aircraft to make the transition from vertical take-off to horizontal flight.
2. American Ryan X-13 Vertijet (1955) The first jet to take off vertically, fly horizontally and then land vertically.

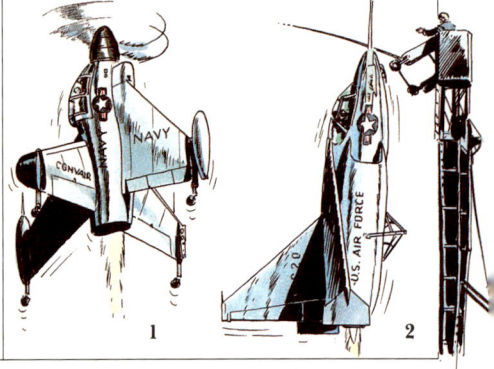

The Hawker Siddeley Harrier

This has just one jet engine, with four pivoting nozzles to help in vertical take-off. The Harrier and the Russian Yakovlev Yak-38 Forger fighter (1972) are the only vertical take-off and landing (VTOL) aircraft still in use. They can operate from makeshift airfields.

American Boeing E-3 AWACS

Eyes in the sky

Some aircraft carry a radar rotodome on top of the fuselage, enabling the crew to watch the movements of ships and aircraft in the area which they are patrolling. Aircraft with this equipment are called AWACS (Airborne Warning And Control System). They are the Boeing E-3 (USA), the Tupolev Tu-126 (USSR) and the Grumman E-2 Hawkeye (USA).

British Hawker Siddeley Harrier (1969)

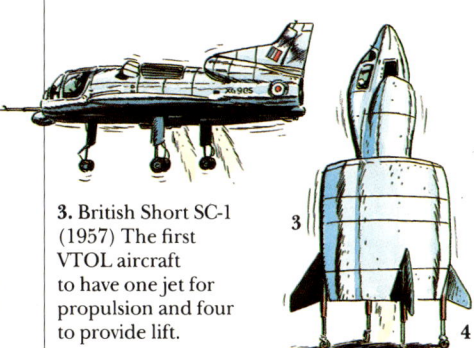

3. British Short SC-1 (1957) The first VTOL aircraft to have one jet for propulsion and four to provide lift.

4. SNECMA C-450 (1959) a French aeroplane with a circular wing

In-flight refuelling

A Blackbird being refuelled through a line dropped from a Boeing KC-135 (the tanker version of the 707).

The first in-flight refuelling took place on 26 June 1923, above San Diego in California. A D.H.4 refuelled another D.H.4 through a pipe.

As aircraft design becomes more sophisticated, aircraft have been developed which can fly vast distances without refuelling.

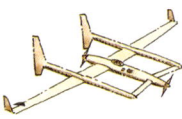

Burt Rutan's Voyager, for instance, was the first to fly non-stop round the world – a distance of 40,212 km. It took him from 14 till 23 December 1986.

The distance that an aeroplane can fly without refuelling depends on the size of its fuel-tanks. Aeroplanes whose tanks are too small can be refuelled in the air by tanker aircraft. This is a spectacular operation; a telescopic antenna joins the two aircraft, and up to 1,000 litres of fuel can be pumped along it while the planes fly less than 10 metres apart at 900 kph.

An alternative to refuelling is to carry the short-haul aeroplane on another, larger, craft for part of the flight.

In 1938 a Short S.25 flying-boat, the *Maia*, carried a Short S.20 seaplane, the *Mercury*, and its cargo of mail for part of the journey from Ireland to Montreal.

In 1944 the German air force took up this idea. To destroy an enemy target a fighter plane, with its pilot, would be attached to the top of an unmanned bomber filled with explosives. The pilot steered the two planes to the target, and then unhooked his fighter. The bomber plummeted down and exploded.

The Leduc 010 prototype is carried up by the four-engined Sud-Est S.E.161 *Languedoc*, on 19 November 1946. It had to reach a speed of 300 kph before it could fly.

The Short aircraft combination *Maia* and *Mercury*

Space shuttles were carried in the same way during their trials, Russian shuttles on an Antonov AN-225 and American ones on a Boeing 747.

The American space shuttle on a Boeing 747

Through the sound to the heat barrier

As more powerful engines were developed, aircraft wings were swept back and made thinner to increase speed. But no-one really believed that a plane could ever travel faster than

The Bell X-1 is propelled by four rockets, and carries enough fuel to last 15 minutes.

On 14 October 1947, Charles (Chuck) Yeager broke through the sound barrier.

the speed of sound (1,193 kph). Airspeeds at this level are measured in Mach; Mach 1 is equal to the speed of sound.

Then the American government started work on a rocket-powered research aircraft, the Bell X-1, and Chuck Yeager, an air force pilot, was chosen to man it.

The aircraft was dropped from a converted bomber at 30,000 feet,

to save fuel. Yeager did a number of flights and each time came closer to the speed of sound, though the aircraft buckled under hammering blows that would have shattered a weaker machine. But Yeager was fully confident in the design of the plane and continued to try.

On 14 October 1947 he opened the four-chamber rocket engine to full power. The needle on the Machmeter swung slowly round past Mach .94 to .96, .98 and the hammering stopped. Yeager had reached the calmer conditions beyond the 'sound barrier'.

More was to follow. In 1953 Yeager, still flying a Bell X-1, reached Mach 2.43. At 2,640 kph he encountered the heat barrier, when the skin of the aircraft's fuselage becomes distorted, and metals melt.

Aircraft were now flying unbelievably fast and high, equipped with immensely powerful engines, and built from new materials which could withstand great speeds and very high temperatures. The next stage was obvious: a machine which could withstand temperatures of 4,000 degrees Celsius would be able to leave and re-enter the Earth's atmosphere. The race for space had begun.

On 7 March 1961 the X-15 flew at Mach 4.43. On 30 March it reached a height of 155,000 feet. Joe Walker, the pilot, experienced weightlessness; he found that he just floated, slowly and gently, unable to control where he went.

Pressurised suit, designed to protect the human body from the effects of speed and altitude

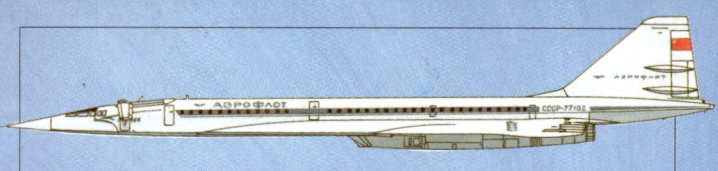

The Tupolev Tu-144 first flew on 31 December 1968. It can carry 167 passengers and has a range of 62,000 km. The nose of the aircraft drops at take-off and landing so that the pilot can see better.

Military aircraft were the first to reach supersonic speeds, but civil aircraft soon followed suit.

Today, New York is only 3¼ hours away from London! In 65 years, aviation has progressed from the Wright brothers' *Flyer*, 200 kg of wood and canvas, to supersonic airliners, 180,000 kg of advanced alloys, which fly at above Mach 2, at an altitude of 55,000 feet.

Supersonic airliners

Only two supersonic airliners have ever been built: the Russian Tupolev Tu-144, and the joint British and French project, Concorde.
On 21 January 1976, a British-owned Concorde set up a new record; it flew across the Atlantic four times in one day.

Concorde, jointly made by BAC (British Aircraft Corporation) and the French company Sud-Aviation, first flew on 2 March 1969. It can carry 144 passengers. Like the Tupolev Tu-144, its nose is lowered for take-off and landing.

Dreaming of space...

Writers began fantasizing about space-travel long before it ever seemed possible. As early as 1649 Cyrano de Bergerac wrote a novel describing a journey in space, called *A Voyage to the Moon*.

Serious science-fiction writing first appeared during the second half of the 19th century. In 1865 the French novelist Jules Verne started a society for the study of space-travel. He wrote various books about imaginary journeys, including *From the Earth to the Moon* (1873). In 1898 H.G. Wells wrote *The War of the Worlds*, followed by *The First Men in the Moon* (1901).

Jules Verne suggested a 'space gun' as a way of catapulting his star voyager to the Moon. We now know that he would be crushed to death by the tremendous forces of gravity without the protection of a machine like the ones astronauts travel in, made of very strong and heat-resistant materials.

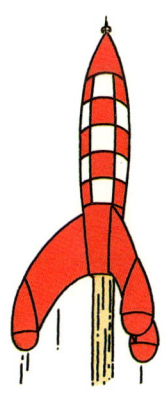

Jules Verne and H.G. Wells inspired Georges Méliès to produce the first science-fiction film, *Journey to the Moon*, in 1902, and space-travel has continued to fascinate film-makers and audiences ever since.

Even Hergé's Tintin went to the moon, during his adventures in *Destination Moon* and *Explorers on the Moon*.

In orbit

Entering orbit
If you throw a stone horizontally from the top of a mountain, the distance it travels before falling to the ground is determined by the force of your throw. If you could only throw it hard enough (7.8 km/sec.) it would travel right round the Earth – it would be in orbit.

The physicist R. H. Goddard (1882–1945)

The stone would be held in orbit by the pull of the Earth's gravity, just as the planets are held in orbit by the Sun's gravitational pull. But if the stone were launched at 11 km/sec., it would not go into orbit; it would leave the atmosphere and go into space.

The earliest space research was carried out by physicists working in laboratories. As long ago as 1883, the Russian Konstantin Tsiolkovsky (1857–1935) discovered that rockets could be fired into space by using the power of a chemical reaction. He devised a rocket fired by liquid propellants, which is the design still used today. He also invented multi-stage rockets, and predicted interplanetary travel and manned space-stations. The Earth, he said, was the cradle of humanity, but he felt the time had come to leave our cradle.

The first modern rocket was launched on 16 March 1926 by the American physicist R.H. Goddard. It was launched at a height of 12 m, rose 56 m and travelled at 96 kph.

Rocket research in pre-war Germany was led by Wernher von Braun (1912–77), who was also responsible for designing the terrible V.2s used in the Second World War. He later moved to America, where

The first space-walker, Alexis Leonov, spent 27 hours in orbit before returning to Earth.

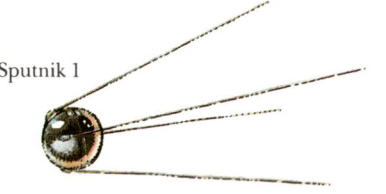

Sputnik 1

he became a leader in the space research programme.

On 4 October 1957 the USSR launched the first satellite to orbit the earth: Sputnik I, which weighed 83.6 kg.

On 3 November 1957, Sputnik II carried the first living creature into space, a small dog called Laika.

The Russian Yuri Gagarin became the first man to orbit the Earth on 12 April 1961, in Vostok 1. The first to leave his spaceship and float freely in space was another Russian Alexis Leonov, in Voskhod II on 18 March 1965.

Yuri Gagarin

Nowadays, rockets regularly fire satellites into orbit. These satellites can send back information which enables scientists to study the Earth's resources and weather patterns. Satellites can also be used to improve communications – you may even have satellite TV at home.

Saturn B rocket (**1**) used to launch the Apollo 11 spacecraft (**2**).
a. 1st stage S.I
b. 2nd stage S.II
c. 3rd stage S.IVB
d. lunar module
e. service module
f. command module

Apollo 11

On 16 July 1969, Apollo 11 took off from Cape Kennedy, Florida. It was 111 m tall, weighed 2,770 tonnes, and had an extra 3,400 tonnes of thrust on take-off. At 9.32 a.m. local time, the astronauts felt the spacecraft shake itself. They were on their way.

There were three astronauts squeezed into the spacecraft: Neil Armstrong, Michael Collins and Edwin Aldrin, all aged 38. They were going to the moon. Their speed of 16 km/sec. would carry them out of the Earth's atmosphere. As Apollo sped onwards, it separated from the various stages of the launching rocket.

Three days later, on 19 July Apollo 11 was in orbit round the moon. On 20 July Armstrong and Aldrin entered the lunar module, Eagle, to go down to the moon, while Collins stayed in orbit. 'OK Eagle... You guys take care,' warned Collins. 'See you later,' Armstrong replied.

The moon is at an average distance of 384,400 km from the Earth.

On 14 September 1959 the Russian lunar probe Luna 2 landed on the moon – the first craft to do so without being destroyed.

Men on the moon
Twelve Americans have set foot on the moon: Armstrong, Aldrin, Conrad, Bean, Sheppard, Mitchell, Scott, Irwin, Young, Duke, Schmitt and Cernan.

From left to right:
Neil Armstrong, Michael Collins and Edwin E. Aldrin Jr.

Men on the moon

On 20 July 1969, at 4.05 p.m., the Eagle slowed down from 6,000 to 4 kph, ready to land on the moon. The module landed at the Sea of Tranquillity, and Armstrong contacted Earth: 'The Eagle has landed.' At 10.38 p.m. the hatch was opened, and Neil Armstrong went out through it.
As he set foot on the

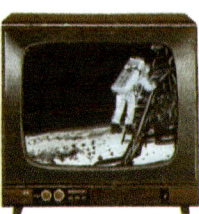

moon's surface, he made the famous comment: 'That's one small step for a man, one giant leap for mankind.'

Armstrong and Aldrin were taken with the Moon. 'It has a stark beauty all its own,' Armstrong told the television public on Earth. 'It's like the high desert of much of the United States. It's different, but it's very pretty here.'

They left a message on the moon for any future visitors to find. It says that men came in peace to the moon, and first walked on its surface in July 1969.

Hermes, the European space-shuttle.

Columbia on its mobile launch-pad, with its accelerators. On take-off it is propelled by two boosters, which are mounted on either side of the huge tanks that provide the shuttle with the liquid fuels (oxygen and hydrogen) it needs in order to fly.

On 17 September 1976 the Enterprise, the first space-shuttle, was presented to the American public. A space-shuttle is a cross between an

Space-shuttles

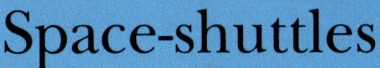

Boran, the Russian space-shuttle

The space-shuttle Columbia: its cabin can carry as many as 12 astronauts. This American shuttle made its first space flight on 12 April 1981. On 11 November 1982 it started its commercial career by carrying into space two telecommunications satellites.

aeroplane and a rocket, and is designed for regular transport between Earth and space. Unlike a rocket, the shuttle can be re-used, to ferry equipment and maintenance crews, and to launch satellites and probes.

Carrying passengers and cargoes into space has become a competitive commercial activity. The European Ariane rocket is much in demand to launch the shuttles: on 22 January 1990 it made its 35th successful launch.

The space-travellers

Houston, America has found some fair winds and some following seas, and we're on our way home . . . We're looking back at some place, I think, we will use as a stepping-stone to go beyond some day . . . It has been a beginning. I don't think there will ever be an end, not as long as man is alive and willing.

Gene Cernan
Commander, Apollo 17
7–19 December 1972

An A to Z of Aircraft Facts

Aerodrome
An open area of land, from which aircraft can take off and land safely. An airport is a more sophisticated place, equipped to handle large airliners.

Aeronaut
The pilot of a balloon, or aerostat.

Alphabet
When a pilot talks to the staff in the control-tower, it is essential that they understand each other perfectly. The ordinary names of some letters of the alphabet sound very similar, so special names are used instead.
Here is the International Phonetic Alphabet:
A Alpha
B Bravo
C Charlie
D Delta
E Echo
F Foxtrot
G Golf
H Hotel
I India
J Juliet
K Kilo
L Lima
M Mike
N November
O Oscar
P Papa
Q Quebec
R Romeo
S Sierra
T Tango
U Uniform
V Victory
W Whisky
X X-ray
Y Yankee
Z Zulu

Anti-G suit
At high speeds, a pilot can be subjected to enormous centrifugal forces which may cause him to lose consciousness. To prevent this, he wears a special flying-suit, with pockets of air which inflate automatically, squeezing the pilot's legs and abdomen to maintain the blood supply to his brain.

Balloon
The canopy of a modern balloon is made of special nylon fabric and polyurethane (made from aluminium) to protect the cloth from heat. It is extremely closely woven, with interlocking threads, so that a small tear does not easily turn into a large hole.

Charter flights
A charter aircraft is hired out for a particular flight. Fares on charter flights can be low because every seat is occupied. There are

companies whose whole business is the hiring and filling of these aircraft.

Control-tower
This is the nerve-centre of any airfield, large or small. In the control-tower are the air-traffic controllers, or the air force personnel who do the same job. In the early days of flying, the control-tower staff could only check whether it looked safe for an aircraft to land. With modern equipment, however, such as radio and radar, the control-tower staff can help aircraft land safely in almost any conditions.

Controlled air space
Large passenger aircraft travel along corridors marked out on maps of the sky, like huge motorways. Other areas are reserved for military planes. The air-space above all airports, however small, is controlled to avoid accidents. Light aircraft can fly wherever they like, but must avoid all the controlled corridors.

Delta-wing
A triangular-shaped wing is called a delta-wing, after the Greek letter delta.

Displays
Sometimes flying displays are part of a big airshow, but teams like the Red Arrows also perform at fairs and carnivals. Some displays are to show the pilots' skill, while others are demonstration flights by new aircraft.

Dog-fight
A dog-fight is an air battle between two planes, with the pilots circling round and attacking each other like dogs. Modern fighters, though, are too fast for dog-fights.

Ejector-seat
A safety-device which enables the pilot to escape from an aircraft in danger of crashing.
It is no longer practical for pilots to wear parachutes all the time, but the ejector-seat has a built-in parachute, as well as a rocket-motor to thrust the pilot at high speed away from the crashing aircraft.

Flying school
Air forces train their own pilots, but people who want to fly civilian planes, whether small private aircraft or huge airliners, must go to a flying school.

G
The unit for measuring centrifugal force. Air force pilots who accelerate fiercely or perform rapid manoeuvres are subjected to great centrifugal force. The Earth's normal gravity is 1G; at 3G the pilot becomes three times his normal weight, and so on.
When a pilot loops the loop at high speed, the force acting on him is at least 4G. As the aircraft turns, the pilot is pushed downwards in his seat, and the blood all goes to the lower part of his body. At 5 or 6G the brain becomes short of blood, and the pilot can no longer see what he is doing. If the aircraft turns right over during a manoeuvre, all the blood rushes to the upper part of his body, with equally uncomfortable results. This is where his anti-G suit comes in.

Gravity
The physical phenomenon which pulls everything towards the centre of the Earth.

Inertial navigation system
A computer system which pinpoints the exact position of the aircraft at all times.

Kilotonne
The unit for measuring the force of an atomic explosion.
1 kilotonne = 1,000 tonnes of TNT.

Mach
The unit based on the speed of sound (1,193 kph), named after the Austrian physicist Ernst Mach. Mach 2 is twice the speed of sound and so on.

N.A.S.A.
National Aeronautics and Space Administration. This American body, founded in 1958, coordinated research into space exploration and aircraft design.

Orbit
The curved path of any object round another object in space. A satellite travelling around the Earth is in orbit.

74

Parachute

The classical shape for the canopy of a parachute is a hemisphere, but other shapes are possible. A modern parachute has slots in the canopy, and steering-wires, so that it can fly both horizontally and vertically. Parachuting is now a sport, as well as a means of escape. Some modern sporting parachutes are more like kites; they are made of tubes of fabric which fill with air.

Police

A modern police force uses aircraft for various purposes. It is easier to observe a traffic-jam building up, and to suggest ways of preventing it, if you are in the air above, not stuck down below in the traffic.

Power produced by a jet-engine

This is called the thrust of the engine, and is measured as weight. The Airbus A320 has two jets, each of which provides 11,300 kg of power.

Profile

The profile or external shape of an aircraft is very important. A smooth, streamlined shape offers least resistance to the air, and so reduces drag. Wings are designed to give as much lift as possible.

Propellant

Rocket fuel, made up of substances which react chemically together to cause the combustion which drives the rocket. The propellant can be liquid or solid.

Satellite

An object in space orbiting around another object. Satellites may be natural (planets) or artificial (launched from Earth for a particular purpose). The zero gravity inside satellite laboratories is permitting all kinds of new scientific research to take place.

Sonic

This means 'to do with sound'. A subsonic aircraft flies below the speed of sound, while a supersonic aircraft flies faster than sound.

Strategic weapons

A strategic nuclear air force consists of bombers or missiles equipped with appallingly powerful nuclear weapons.

Tactical weapons

A tactical nuclear air force consists of aircraft which carry small nuclear weapons, designed to be dropped on specific targets.

Vertical take-off

Taking off straight into the air, without using a runway.

About the author

James Prunier's family acquired its first television set in 1969, just in time to watch Armstrong and Aldrin walking on the moon. James Prunier has always been up in the clouds, if not quite on the moon. This is perhaps why the French Académie de l'Air et de l'Espace gave him a Bronze Medal in 1989. Or was it because he is so good at making aeroplane noises to entertain his small daughter? His next job is to teach her to make paper aeroplanes.

The author would like to thank Jean-Marie Boule and the training base at Tours, Jean-Marc Culas, Sylvie and Patrice Doyotte, Philippe Hubert, Patrick Singer, and especially Edmond Petit, Pierre Clostermann and the Musée de l'Air et de l'Espace at Le Bourget for their help in producing the four volumes of this History of Aviation.

A HISTORY OF AVIATION

Collect the other 3 volumes in this series, each one with text and illustrations by James Prunier

Vol.1 Pioneers of the Air
Vol.2 Flying Aces
Vol.3 Fighters

Other titles in the *Discoverers* series:

Discovering the seasons:
**Spring
Summer
Autumn
Winter**

Discovering nature:
**Your Cat
The Book of the Sky
The Book of Rivers
The Book of the Forest
The Book of Deserts
The Book of Mountains
Flowers**

Discovering history:
**The Book of Inventions and Discoveries
Clothes Through the Ages
Uniforms Through the Ages
Ships and Seafarers
Conquerors and Invaders
Navigators and Explorers
Land Exploration
Traders and Trade Routes**

Discovering transport:
**The Story of Trains
Pioneers of the Sky
Flying Aces
Fighters**

Discovering art:
Painting and Painters